Amazing Journeys

School Specialty
Publishing
Columbus, Ohio

By Katharine Kenah

Copyright © 2007 School Specialty Publishing, a member
of the School Specialty Family.

Library of Congress Cataloging-in-Publication Data is on file with the publisher.

Send all inquiries to:
School Specialty Publishing
8720 Orion Place
Columbus, OH 43240-2111

ISBN 0-7696-4337-X

1 2 3 4 5 6 7 8 9 10 PHX 10 09 08 07 06

Some animals live in one place.
Some animals move from place to place.
They move to find food.
They move to find warm weather.
They move to find safety.
Animals that move migrate.
Some animals take amazing journeys!

Arctic Tern

Arctic terns are on the move!
They fly from the top of the world
to the bottom—and back—every year.
The distance is equal to circling
the earth one time.

Canada Goose

Canada geese are on the move!
A flock of geese fly in a V shape.
The V shape helps all the birds
stay together.
Canada geese fly north in the spring.
They fly south to warm weather
in the fall.

Starling

Starlings are on the move!
Starlings migrate during the day
and night.
By day, starlings follow rivers
and shorelines.
By night, starlings follow the moon
and stars.
Once a young starling makes its first
migration, it seems to remember
the trip the next time.

Gray Whale

Gray whales are on the move!
In summer, gray whales swim
in cold water near the North Pole.
They eat and store up fat,
called *blubber*.
In winter, they swim south
to the warm water near Mexico.

Sea Turtle

Sea turtles are on the move!
When sea turtles are ready to lay eggs,
they swim over 1,000 miles.
They swim to the beaches
where they were born.
They lay eggs in holes in the sand.
Then, they return to the sea.

14

Salmon

Salmon are on the move!
Salmon are born in streams.
Then, they swim out to the ocean
to live.
When it is time to lay eggs,
some adult salmon swim 2,000 miles
back to the stream where
they were born.

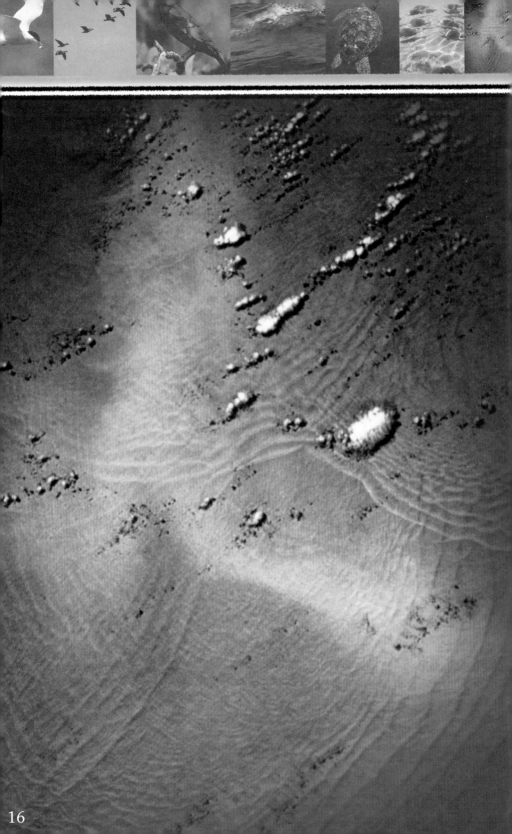

Zooplankton

Zooplankton are on the move!
Zooplankton are very tiny animals.
They live near the top of the sea.
Zooplankton migrate every day.
They swim down
when the sun comes out.
They swim up
when the sky grows dark.

Earthworm

Earthworms are on the move!
During cold weather, earthworms
crawl down deep into the ground.
The dirt is warm and wet there.
In warm weather, they crawl up again.
The dirt is warmer near the surface.

Desert Locust

Desert locusts are on the move!
They move in groups called *swarms*.
One swarm may have billions
of locusts.
This is one locust for almost every
person on earth.
Migrating swarms can grow so large
that they block out the sunlight!

Monarch Butterfly

Monarch butterflies are on the move!
In September, monarch butterflies fly
from Canada to Mexico.
They fly towards warm weather.
In March, monarch butterflies
fly north again.
They fly close to 2,000 miles!

Caribou

Caribou are on the move!
Caribou migrate around
the Arctic Circle.
This is the cold spot
at the top of the world.
Caribou walk hundreds of miles.
They look for food to eat.
They look for places to give birth.

African Elephant

African elephants are on the move!
They migrate over large, grassy spaces.
They look for food and water.
Elephants are called
"gardeners of Africa."
They drop seeds as they eat plants
and move.

Serengeti Migration

Millions of animals are on the move!
The Serengeti is a national park
in Tanzania, Africa.
It is the size of the state of Connecticut!
Zebras, gazelles, and wildebeest
migrate around the park each year.
They move to find food and water.

Bedouin

People are on the move, too!
Bedouins (BEH-du-wins) live in hot,
dry lands.
They live in tents.
They tend herds of animals.
They move to find water and grass
for their animals.

TREME FACTS ABOUT AMAZING JOURNEYS!

- Arctic terns migrate nearly 24,000 miles each year, the greatest distance of any bird.

- Some geese can fly more than 1,000 miles, about the distance from New York to Chicago, without stopping to rest.

- Starlings gather together at night in large groups, called *roosts*. A single roost may have over a million birds.

- Gray whales do not eat much while they are migrating. They may go without food for three to five months.

- The leatherback sea turtle can grow to be 8 feet long and weigh 1,500 pounds, as much as a full-grown moose.

- Scientists think that once salmon reach the coast, they can recognize the smell of their home stream. They follow the scent home.

- Zooplankton swim down several hundred feet during the day, about the length of a 100-story building.

- Earthworms have five pairs of hearts.

- In 1988, a swarm of desert locusts flew 3,105 miles from West Africa to the Caribbean in 10 days without stopping. This is about the distance of flying across the United States.

- Monarch butterflies migrate so regularly that some communities in the United States have festivals to celebrate their return.

- Caribou feet are like snowshoes. They are large and wide, so the caribou can walk in snow.

- Elephants have padded feet, so they can walk and run with little noise.

- Migrating herds of animals in the Serengeti move in a circle in a clockwise direction.

- Dairy products are the main food source for bedouins. They make yogurt and butter from camel and goat milk.